West Yorkshire and Navigat

CW00797916

on old picture pos

Norman Ellis

RIVER AIRE, LEEDS BRIDGE.

No 320

1. This view from **Leeds** Bridge, c.1930, shows the River Aire curving away towards Crown Point. Warehouse Hill Wharf is on the left bank, with extensive warehouses on the right bank. A variety of craft and several cranes are visible. Recent investment has changed the left bank from industrial to residential and commercial use. The postcard was published by H Burniston of Leeds.

Designed and published by Reflections of a Bygone Age, Keyworth, Nottingham, 2009

Printed by Adlard Print & Reprographics, Ruddington, Nottingham

£3.95

Introduction

I was seven years old when my parents first took me walking beside a lovely canal on the outskirts of Wakefield. At about the same period, I occasionally gazed out of our back bedroom window and saw boats moving along another waterway almost two miles away. Years later, I learned that the lovely waterway was the Barnsley Canal near Heath, built to convey coal from South Yorkshire (then part of the West Riding) to Goole. The boats I saw were 'Tom Puddings' near Stanley Ferry, laden with coal and bound for Goole.

I obtained my first job in 1946 at Hepburn Conveyor Company in Wakefield. I realized that I was working in a very old stone building, whose entrance incorporated a pillared porch and pediment. The windows were protected by internal shutters which I had to unbolt and open every morning and close every evening. The inside walls divided the building into three large sections, plus a small reception area. The largest section was the drawing office (where I worked). Another section accommodated the typists and clerks (all female), with the third section being the abode of the managing director. In 1948, the building acquired a tasteless brick addition to house the new drawing office. The factory buildings were a motley collection of old and newer structures of no architectural merit. I left the firm in 1949.

Years later, I discovered that the stone building had belonged to the Aire & Calder Navigation Company. This concern had made the Rivers Aire and Calder navigable up to Leeds and Wakefield in the early 1700s. Joseph Priestley was appointed head clerk to the A & C N in 1816. He controlled its day-to-day running from a building in Navigation Yard, Wakefield - the very building in which I had worked! The original Wakefield terminus of the Aire & Calder Navigation was at the other side of Navigation Yard. After Priestley's retirement in 1851, Leeds became the headquarters of the A & C N. The Wakefield building was honoured with a blue plaque in 2000, the tasteless brick extension by then having been removed to reveal all the original façade. Stylish brick houses adjacent to the office building once housed the families of waterway employees. These buildings were restored in the 1970s.

The town (later city) of Wakefield, which had become established to the north of the River Calder, eventually found itself at the confluence of three waterways. Two of these - The Aire & Calder Navigation and the Calder & Hebble Navigation - were river based, but relied heavily on the construction of diversions and cuts. The third - the Barnsley Canal - was entirely man made. The Calder & Hebble Navigation was really a continuation of the Aire & Calder Navigation at Wakefield, the two being joined at the town's Fall Ings Cut. The C & H N became open throughout its full length to Sowerby Bridge in 1770, where it connected with the Rochdale Canal. The Barnsley Canal was opened in 1799, although a short section beyond Barnsley was not opened until 1802. The A & C N purchased the Barnsley Canal in 1875, having leased it since 1854.

In 1826, the Aire & Calder Navigation opened a section of canal from Knottingley to Goole, together with the Port of Goole, thus allowing much larger craft to move along the various waterways. The Lancashire & Yorkshire Railway was granted access to the port and made vital contributions to its success.

Having taken fifty years to build, the Leeds & Liverpool Canal was finally opened over its full length in 1816, although the Leeds to Gargrave section was operative from 1777, as was the Liverpool to Wigan section. The total length was 127 miles. On the Yorkshire side, 44 locks were constructed, with 47 in Lancashire. Along its length, two tunnels were dug, the Foulridge one being almost a mile long. The Leeds & Liverpool is a true canal, as opposed to a navigation, but on the Yorkshire side of the Pennines, it takes advantage of the Aire Valley.

The main cargoes carried on the West Yorkshire waterways were coal, grain and flour. Also conveyed were stone, sand, cement, iron, timber, paper, textile materials, hides, oil, tar and all manner of foodstuffs, including canned. In 1948, the British Transport Commission took over most of the canals and navigations of Britain, including the Leeds & Liverpool Canal and the Aire & Calder and Calder & Hebble Navigations. By then, the railways had appropriated a lot of the business previously handled by the waterways, much of which subsequently went to road transport. In Yorkshire, the closure of coal mines was a contributory factor in the demise of waterway transportation. The canals and navigations that remain are a unique asset for those who wish to 'mess about' in boats, or simply to walk along the towpaths.

This book is about the canals and navigations in West Yorkshire. The Calder & Hebble is wholly within this region. The Goole end of the Aire & Calder is over the boundary, but is I think justifiably included because of its importance. Similarly, for the Leeds & Liverpool Canal, the Skipton and Gargrave areas, both just outside West Yorkshire (but within the West Riding) are included. The Huddersfield Broad and Huddersfield Narrow Canals receive brief coverage. The postcards are from my own collection, built up over almost forty years.

Boats and Boat People

The pretty images on certain postcards create a false image of some aspects of canal life. For most boat people, the work was hard and unrelenting. Many of the boats belonged to the companies that owned the canals and navigations. But there were numerous by-traders, i.e. separate companies with significant fleets, or individuals with one or two boats. Canal owners obtained part of their revenue from tolls charged to boat operators. The coming of the railways compounded many of the inherent problems on the waterways. One reaction was for skippers to get rid of their mate and boy and bring the family on board to act as crew, perhaps after giving up the home ashore. Life aboard was arduous and cramped, with the children receiving no proper schooling. Boats needed regular maintenance. Horses needed food, water and rest periods, as well as new shoes every few weeks. Winters were particularly difficult when locks or towpaths froze.

To obviate the necessity for horses, the motive power on many craft became the steam-propelled engine. Certain operators also made use of steam tugs for hauling dumb barges, i.e. those without engines. Eventually, diesel units became a feature on many barges. Various types of timber, including English oak, were used for barge construction, but metal-structured boats were introduced in later years.

The living quarters on barges were often made very snug, with an oven in the forward cabin and an open fireplace in the aft one. Folding tables and built-in drawers and cupboards were incorporated; berths could be closed off when not in use. The tasks of a family of father, mother and children were many. Father acted as skipper, but steering the boat was only one of his numerous jobs. Mother was mate and deckhand, keeping the craft tidy, cooking, baking and washing. Children took on responsibilities from an early age. To maintain tight schedules, the whole family were expected to buckle in.

Norman Ellis
February 2009

RIVER AIRE—Looking towards Warehouse Hill Wharf.

2. The terminus of the Leeds & Liverpool Canal and Aire & Calder Navigation is shown near **Leeds** Bridge, c.1912. The latter's actual navigation ended at Crown Point, where the River Aire was met. The backdrop to this view is Warehouse Hill Wharf, the dwarfed building, centre, being the Riverside Mission Hall.

Front cover: This 'West Country' barge, built at Ledgard Bridge Yard, **Mirfield**, is pictured just after launching, moored at the edge of the Calder & Hebble Navigation. 'West Country' boats generally worked west of the River Humber. The dress of the celebratory party suggests c.1908.

Back cover (top): The bridge at Dowley Gap, near **Saltaire**, involved a change of towpath sides for the boatman and horse. The rectangular enclosure close to the bridge is a 'catch pit' to collect sediment from a nearby lane. The Leeds & Liverpool Canal carrier boat, Swallow, appears to have unloaded. The card was posted from Keighley to Ossett in 1905.

Back cover (bottom): This view of the Aire & Calder Navigation's iron aqueduct at **Stanley Ferry**, looking towards the southwest, dates from c.1907. Crossing the River Calder at the point shown, it opened in 1839. Due to mining subsidence, it was replaced by a concrete structure in 1981. Wakefield photographer E I Walker produced the card.

Riverside Mission River Trip—S.S. THOMAS leaving Warehouse Hill Wharf.

3. The Mission Hall on Warehouse Hill Wharf, **Leeds**, catered for the spiritual and social needs of boatmen and their families. Here, the SS Thomas is about to leave the wharf on a trip organised by the mission, c.1912.

Contents

4. Placid reflections feature on this scene of the Leeds & Liverpool Canal at Redcote, **Armley**, c.1920. The bridge formed part of a driveway to Benjamin Gott's country mansion, Armley House. In 1928, the park and house were presented to the City of Leeds, becoming a golf course and club house.

5. The horse-propelled barge, heading through **Rodley** towards Leeds, is gliding past mills on the left and is about to pass the Smith & Booth Crane Works on the right. The card was posted to Buxton on 2 March 1909 with the message, *"We have had a heavy fall of snow here on Sunday and Monday."*

6. A boat, travelling in the Leeds direction on the L & L, is emerging from the two-rise locks at **Apperley Bridge**, as a skipper holds the tiller of *Sydney*, belonging to Bingley coal merchant James Glover, in readiness for the ascent, c.1912. These step locks used more water than frequent single locks and tended to cause delays.

7. This photograph affords a splendid view of part of the same locks at **Apperley Bridge**, probably on the same day. Locally, they were known as the Dobson Locks. The balance beams for opening and closing the 'V' shape lock gates are visible, as are windlasses to operate paddles in the gates.

8. The broadside launch of the pleasure boat *Dawn* is captured on camera beside the boat building yard at Dockfields, **Shipley**, on the Leeds & Liverpool Canal, thought to be 1908.

9. Male onlookers have been quick to jump aboard the newly launched *Dawn* at **Shipley**. The ladies are showing more decorum. The nearness of the railway is indicated by the signals and coaches in the background.

Dubb Bridge Bingley

10. The Leeds & Liverpool Canal is pictured passing beneath Dubb Lane Bridge at **Bingley**, c.1910. Coal is being unloaded from a barge by wheelbarrow. In the distance is the spire of Mornington Road Wesleyan Methodist Church. Much of the property shown has gone; even the bridge has been replaced.

11. Canal locks needed fairly regular maintenance. Here, the famous Five Rise Locks on the Leeds & Liverpool at **Bingley** have been drained to allow for repairs, including replacement of the sills at the base of the top lock, to create seals when the gates are closed. The exact date is uncertain, but probably early 1900s.

12. The Five Rise Locks at **Bingley** were opened with much celebration in 1774. The first official boat took 28 minutes to descend. These locks lift the canal 60 feet; the nearby Three Rise Locks another 30 feet. The photograph dates from c.1912.

13. A heavily laden barge is emerging from the lower end of Three Rise Locks at **Bingley**, c.1925. The towing horse (with nose in bucket), having been led down the towpath, left, is about to resume its duties. The lock-keeper's cottage is visible at the top. Bradford photographer B Matthews issued the card.

14. Leach's Swing Bridge is pictured on the Leeds & Liverpool Canal at **Riddlesden**, near Keighley. Although space looks limited, the boat would pass through with relative ease. Lilywhite of Halifax produced the postcard.

15. Interesting canal side architecture and accoutrements feature on this card of the L & L Canal at **Kildwick**, posted from nearby Cross-Hills to Headingley Hill, Leeds, in August 1905. In the distance, the towpath disappears under Parson's Bridge.

16. This is Parson's Bridge at **Kildwick** in c.1922, viewed from the opposite side to the previous photograph. The Leeds-registered barge has attracted a few onlookers on the bridge. The horse is apparently resting on the right.

17. Main Street at **Farnhill** looks dangerously close to the Leeds & Liverpool Canal, although perhaps only the cellars (some are visible) of the houses would be vulnerable to flooding. In the distance is Kildwick Church. The card was posted from Keighley to Thornbury, Bradford, in 1906, requesting a silver pencil case.

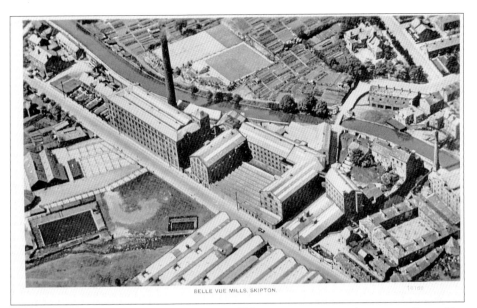

BELLE VUE MILLS, SKIPTON.

18. Belle Vue Mills on Broughton Road, **Skipton**, were erected as a woollen mill in 1828. After a disastrous fire in 1831, the complex was rebuilt as a cotton mill, and enlarged several times. The L & L Canal, which facilitated deliveries of raw cotton from Liverpool, is seen curving around the rear of the buildings in this c.1930 shot.

19. A flyboat is moored at the **Skipton** basin, with eighteenth century L & L buildings in the background (Belmont Bridge off the picture to the right). Coal, cotton and provisions were brought to Skipton by canal; limestone was taken out. The town's photographer, John Henry Smith, produced the card, c.1910.

20. In June1908, a violent thunderstorm, lasting two hours, broke over the hills above **Skipton**. Areas of the town became flooded. Here, beside Canal Street, the Springs Canal (a branch of the L & L in Skipton) has burst its banks and is flowing into the Eller Beck.

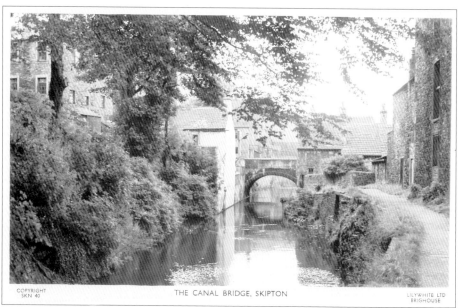

THE CANAL BRIDGE, SKIPTON

21. Springs Canal at **Skipton**, depicted here, was constructed in 1773 as part of a scheme to transport limestone from the quarries behind the castle. It entered the town at Mill Bridge, also shown. The old corn mill at extreme right gave the bridge its name. Lilywhite of Brighouse published the card.

22. These are company flyboats, which often worked around the clock, usually operated by three or four people, all of whom may have been part of the same family. Note the barrels of drinking water. The location is **Gargrave** on the L & L, and the card, by Airton's Studio, Park Place, Gargrave, was posted from there in 1905.

23. This wintry scene at **Gargrave** is from almost the same vantage point, c.1905, and shows the Leeds & Liverpool Canal frozen over. Men, special boats and horses were sometimes brought in to break the ice, but progress was difficult.

24. In all, six locks were constructed at **Bank Newton**, near Gargrave, to raise the L & L a total of 50 feet, bringing it to 400 feet above sea level. A maintenance boat rests adjacent to a carpenters' work yard, part of the Bank Newton maintenance depot. The card, published by Thomas Turner, stationer, Skipton, was posted in 1912.

25. The double bridge at **East Marton** results from the building of a new road along the route of the A 59. The lower bridge, probably dating from 1772, carried the old turnpike. It was not considered adequate for later heavy traffic. The card was posted from East Marton in 1912.

Greenbrierfield Locks.

Clough & Wells
Nile Series

381

26. The ascent of the L & L at **Greenbrierfield** (to 487 feet above sea level) is exemplified in this c.1920 scene, water being supplied by a pipe from Winterburn Reservoir nine miles away. The original three-lock staircase was re-routed through three separate locks (part shown here) in 1828. Skipton postcard publishers Clough & Wells produced the view.

SALTERFORTH BRIDGE.

27. *"When are you coming to see me?",* wrote Betty when she posted this card of the Leeds & Liverpool Canal at **Salterforth** to Miss Holden at Haslingden, Lancashire, in 1911. The name Salterforth suggests a ford on a medieval salt way from Cheshire to the northeast of England.

OLD STYLE.

NEW STYLE.

LEEDS TERMINUS.

TOWING COAL COMPARTMENT BOATS.

HYDRAULIC COAL HOIST.

28. This correspondence card was issued by the Aire & Calder Navigation from their **Leeds** headquarters. It encapsulates the company's history from horse barges to compartment boats, some of the latter being known as 'Tom Puddings'. Carrying coal, they plied between Stanley Ferry, near Wakefield, and Goole. The same illustration, with its delightful montages, was utilized by the A & C on other publicity material.

WAKEFIELD BRIDGE

29. The River Calder, shown here from the east in the early 1900s, performed an important part in the development of **Wakefield**. The river was dammed in the thirteenth century (visible through the arches of Chantry Bridge) to direct water towards waterwheels at the mill on the right. Wakefield photographers G & J Hall produced the card.

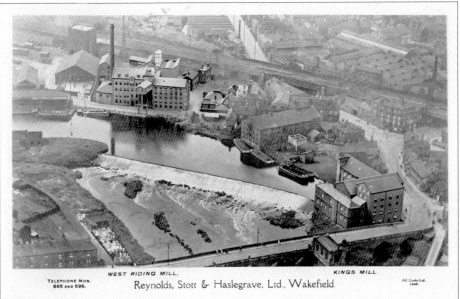

WEST RIDING MILL.   KINGS MILL.

TELEPHONE NOS.
595 AND 596.   Reynolds, Stott & Haslegrave, Ltd., Wakefield.   Alf. Cooke Ltd.
                                                                              Leeds

30. This aerial view of the Calder at **Wakefield** shows a different aspect of the buildings in the top picture, c.1920. Alf Cooke Ltd, the Leeds printers, produced the card for Reynolds, Stott & Haslegrave, flour millers at West Riding Mill and King's Mill, both illustrated. The expanse of water above the weir became known as 'The Pond'.

31. Fall Ings Cut at **Wakefield**, pictured here c.1904, was opened in 1761 by the Calder & Hebble Navigation Company. It diverged from the River Calder beneath the footbridge shown, continued under the Doncaster and Barnsley Roads and emerged opposite Thornes Lane Wharf beside 'The Pond', thus bypassing unnavigable sections of the Calder.

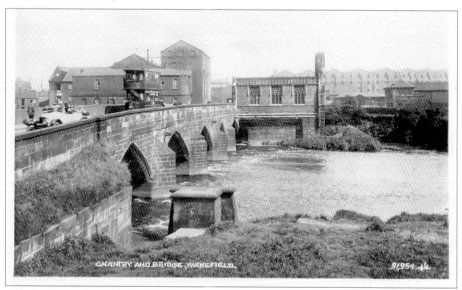

32. In the early 1700s, the Alre & Calder Navigation Company constructed a cut (later named Old Cut) from about 600 yards downstream from Chantry Bridge, **Wakefield**, pictured here. It terminated in Navigation Yard, visible in the distance to right of the chapel. This original cut was replaced by Fall Ings (or New) Cut. Valentines of Dundee published the card.

33. To compete with the railway, Tom Pudding compartment boats were introduced by the A & C Navigation in 1865, to deliver West Riding coal to Goole. Each boat was loaded with coal at St John's Colliery, Wakefield, and shunted by rail to Newland Basin at **Stanley Ferry**, to be lowered into the water, as shown.

34. Tom Puddings, filled with coal, are passing along the A & C Navigation near **Stanley**. Behind the tug is a false bow to prevent water from the propeller building up in front of the first container. A crew of four is visible. Both these postcards were issued by Wakefield photographer H M Wilson, c.1912.

THE AQUEDUCT, STANLEY FERRY

35. The iron aqueduct at **Stanley Ferry** was opened by the Aire & Calder Navigation in 1839. It is featured on a quiet day in the 1950s, looking towards Altofts Bridge. A replacement concrete structure was opened to the right in 1981. Compartment boats were repaired in workshops visible on the left.

Ryhill, near Wakefield

36. To ensure a guaranteed depth of water on the Barnsley Canal, feeder reservoirs were constructed at Cold Hiendley and Wintersett, near **Ryhill**. The latter reservoir is pictured on the right, viewed from near the railway station and signal box at Ryhill. The card was posted from there in 1923.

37. The Barnsley Canal was opened in 1799 for transportation of coal from the Barnsley and Silkstone areas. It entered the River Calder near the later-constructed cooling towers at Wakefield (now demolished). This is Lover's Bridge on the canal near **Heath**, on a postcard by Judges of Hastings.

38. Stone Heaps Bridge, pictured here c.1908, crossed the Barnsley Canal at **Walton**, near Wakefield. Dynamite was used to blast out the cutting. The view belies the fact that this was an industrial waterway, although a barge is visible in the distance. Abandonment for commercial use came in 1953.

39. The town of **Castleford**, built on the banks of the River Aire, became a busy manufacturing centre. At Castleford, the Calder loses its identity when it joins the Aire, shown on the right, looking south. An entrance to the cut is visible beneath the footbridge, left, with another behind the houses.

40. Skirting the town's north side, the **Castleford** Cut was constructed by the Aire & Calder Navigation to bypass the winding Aire. Here, on the right, is Castleford Middle Lock, with Bullholme Lock and the railway bridge in the distance. Both these cards were posted in 1904, being the work of H Graham Glen, Wortley, Leeds.

41. The chemical works at **Castleford** are featured beside the River Aire, but near the A & Cs Castleford Cut. Hickson & Partners moved to the premises c.1915. The firm later became Hickson & Welch. During the wars, high explosives were produced. The card, by William Bramley, Cross Gates, was posted in 1914.

42. A train of Tom Puddings, carrying coal and probably bound for Goole, is caught passing beneath the railway bridge at **Brotherton**, on a navigable part of the River Aire. General merchandise is being towed in the opposite direction. The postcard dates from c.1910.

43. Ferrybridge 'A' Power Station, pictured here, was opened in 1927. The card, by E L Scrivens of Doncaster, was produced a few years later. The bridge, now an ancient monument, was built to carry the Great North Road over the Aire. Ferrybridge 'B' and 'C' Power Stations were opened in 1957 and 1967 respectively.

44. The Knottingley & Goole Canal features on this photograph, taken at The Junction, **Knottingley**, c.1907, with the toll office on the right. Beyond Trundles Lane Bridge, left, is Bank Dole Cut (running via a section of the River Aire to the Selby Canal). On its right bank is the tar distillery.

THE CANAL KNOTTINGLEY

45. In 1826, vessels started using the newly-constructed Knottingley & Goole Canal (part of the A & C, it actually started at Ferrybridge). It ran generally parallel with, but further south than the River Aire. This view of the canal is from Jackson's Bridge, **Knottingley**, looking east. The postcard, by W Bramley of Cross Gates, was issued c.1910.

COPYRIGHT KTY 10   THE BENDELS, KNOTTINGLEY   LILYWHITE LTD BRIGHOUSE

46. From the same vantage point at **Knottingley** half a century later, the details are somewhat changed. The limestone staithes have gone. The ground to the right (an area called The Bendles) is dominated by Bagley's glass bottle works, later to become part of Rockware. The postcard was published by Lilywhite of Brighouse.

47. The Port of **Goole** was opened in 1826. The A & C allowed the Lancashire & Yorkshire Railway to make Goole its eastern terminus in 1848. This busy postcard, published by H G Glen of Leeds in c.1905, illustrates one of several hoists used to lift Tom Puddings out of the water and tip their coal into ships' holds.

48. Numerous Tom Pudding compartment boats, carrying different types of coal, are visible on this view of Ouse Dock, **Goole**. Observe the numbers on the boats. The postcard, by Arjay Productions of Doncaster, probably dates from the 1950s.

49. A horse-drawn barge is heading along the Calder & Hebble Navigation between the two Broad Cut Locks at Calder Grove, **Wakefield**. At extreme right is a coal staithe for discharging from wagon to boat. Photographer H M Wilson of Wakefield produced the card, c.1912.

50. The C & H Old Cut at **Horbury Bridge**, just north of the Calder, is shown, looking towards Horbury Bridge Mill (woollen) and Old Mill (mungo). The tract between river and cut became known as 'The Island'. The replacement New Cut, south of the river, was opened in 1738. The card, published by Alfred Kershaw, local newsagent, was posted in 1928.

51. The Calder & Hebble Navigation at **Thornhill** was crossed by this viaduct, here under construction for the Midland Railway in 1905. This rail branch ran to Savile Town, Dewsbury. The Midland's ambitious plans to take the line to Bradford (from near Barnsley) failed to materialize.

52. A 'West Country' type barge is negotiating the upper lock at Double Locks at **Thornhill**. The location is the same as the top picture, but later. 'West Country' boats were of a size to work west of the Humber and popular on the A & C and C & H. This family barge (father, mother, daughter visible?) is probably carrying perishables.

53. The Aire & Calder Company enjoyed close liaison with the Calder & Hebble Company and constructed its own basin at **Savile Town**, Dewsbury. Part of this is shown here, together with the adjacent saw mills of William Hodgson & Sons. The card was published by A Sunderland of Savile Town.

GREENWOOD LOCK, RAVENSTHORPE

54. Locks and lock-keepers' cottages were attractive features of many canals and navigations, including the Calder & Hebble, as exemplified by this picture of Greenwood Lock on Greenwood Cut, **Ravensthorpe**, c.1925. Note the pigeon loft. W C Machan, fancy goods dealer, Wakefield, published the card.

GREENWOOD LOCK, RAVENSTHORPE.

55. Greenwood Lock at **Ravensthorpe** is again shown, c.1925, with the lock-keeper's cottage and towpath on the right. Parts of Mirfield are visible in the distance. The card was published by Allen & Sons, wholesale newsagents of Oldham.

56. Steanard Lane is pictured, leading up to Shepley Bridge, **Ravensthorpe**. The actual bridge crosses the River Calder near a malt house. On the left, barges are visible at the lock entrance to a dry dock and the Shepley Bridge Cut of the Calder & Hebble. The card was posted from Dewsbury to Rhyl in 1908.

57. In the early hours of 15 April 1909, Stott's four-storey flour mill at **Mirfield**, leased from the Calder & Hebble Navigation, caught fire. Appliances from Dewsbury, Huddersfield and Mirfield attended, but the mill was largely destroyed, placing sixty employees out of work. Note the barge on the right.

58. Upriver from Mirfield, the next stretch of navigation was the **Battyeford** Cut, where a boatbuilding yard was established by the C & H. It is shown here, looking east, c.1928. The boat, to a later design, has a slatted cover over the hold.

BRIGHOUSE—THE CANAL AT THE LANDING WHARFE.

59. The large basins at **Brighouse** were constructed to serve the town, but were also the terminus of a wagonway from the Clifton Coalfield. This 1920s view shows a loaded vessel passing through a lock into the lower basin, assisted by a horse. The card was published by Walter Scott of Bradford.

Brookfoot, Brighouse.

60. The River Calder and a stretch of the Calder & Hebble Navigation feature on this panorama of Brookfoot, near **Brighouse**, looking towards Elland, c.1910. On the right-hand bank of the navigation, stone blocks and slabs are visible, brought from neighbouring quarries for shipment along the waterway.

61. A barge is moored at Woodside, **Elland**, beside a modest building provided for boat people, complete with baking and washing facilities. Looming large behind are Woodside Flour Mills, where boats delivered coal and grain and collected flour for transit along the C & H.

62. *"Do you know the place? Just guess who has sent it"*, reads the message on the back of the card. It was posted from Halifax to Golcar in 1906 and shows the lovely lock cottage on the C & H at **Salterhebble**, near Halifax. The Lancashire & Yorkshire Railway line is in the near background.

23148   THE CANAL, COPLEY, HALIFAX.

63. The horse-drawn barge at **Copley**, near Halifax, is heading for Sowerby Bridge on the Calder & Hebble Navigation, having just passed beneath Copley Lane Bridge. To the left, on an embankment, is the L & Y Railway. The card was published by W H Smith in their 'Strand' series.

64. At **Sowerby Bridge**, the C & H connected with the Rochdale Canal to provide a through route into Lancashire. On the Rochdale Canal at Sowerby Bridge, a group are preparing for an outing on a boat provided by local carrier, Albert Wood, c.1905. Observe the industrial equipment in the background. Hirst & Co, local photographers, produced the card.